# Thinking Beyond the Task

*The Discipline of Seeing the Bigger Picture at Work*

KISHORE KUMAR THAKUR

## Copyright Page



This book is intended for educational and informational purposes only. The views expressed herein are those of the author and are based on professional experience and reflection. They are not intended as legal, financial, or psychological advice. Readers are encouraged to apply the concepts thoughtfully within their own context and judgment.

ISBN: 978-93-5777-784-1

First Edition: 2026

Published by: KISHORE KUMAR THAKUR
Printed in INDIA

# Table of Contents

# Introduction

## Why Most Work Stays at the Task Level

In most organizations, people are busy. Days are filled with emails, meetings, deadlines, and deliverables. Tasks get completed, reports get submitted, and projects move forward in small steps. Yet, despite this constant activity, many employees feel that their work is largely operational. They are doing what is asked, meeting expectations, and staying productive—yet they sense that something more is expected of them, something often described as "being more strategic."

The challenge is that strategic thinking is rarely defined in a way that feels accessible. It is often associated with senior leadership, long-term planning, or high-level decision-making. As a result, many employees quietly assume that strategic thinking is relevant only when they reach higher positions. Until then, their role seems to be to execute tasks efficiently and reliably.

This assumption creates a subtle but significant limitation. When work is approached only at the level of task completion, employees may become highly effective performers but remain confined within the boundaries of immediate assignments. They respond quickly, deliver consistently, and stay focused on what needs to be done next. However, they may not always see how their work connects to larger goals, future consequences, or broader organizational priorities. Over time, this can create a gap between being recognized as dependable and being perceived as strategic.

The purpose of this book is to bridge that gap.

Strategic thinking is not reserved for a select few at the top of the hierarchy. It is a way of seeing work—of understanding how individual actions relate to wider outcomes, how short-term decisions influence long-term results, and how everyday choices contribute to organizational value. It does not require a change in title or authority. It requires a shift in perspective.

Many capable professionals remain at the task level not because they lack intelligence or ambition, but because their work environments emphasize execution speed over reflective thinking. Deadlines reward quick completion, not always thoughtful consideration of implications. Performance reviews often focus on deliverables achieved rather than value created. In such settings, it becomes natural to concentrate on finishing assigned work rather than asking how that work might influence future outcomes, cross-functional coordination, or customer impact.

Over time, this habit of task-focused thinking can become deeply ingrained. When given an assignment, the immediate question becomes, "What exactly should I do?" rather than, "What outcome is this task meant to influence?" When faced with a problem, the instinct may be to fix the visible issue rather than explore underlying causes or longer-term prevention. When attending meetings, individuals may provide status updates without offering perspectives on risks, trade-offs, or opportunities that extend beyond the immediate scope of discussion.

None of these patterns indicate a lack of capability. They reflect a way of working that has been shaped by daily demands and organizational norms. Yet they also reveal where strategic thinking begins to emerge—not in grand strategic plans, but in small moments of awareness about context, consequence, and connection.

This book is built on a simple premise: strategic thinking can be practiced in everyday work, long before one holds a senior leadership role. It develops when individuals learn to connect their tasks to broader goals, anticipate implications before acting, recognize interdependencies across teams, and make choices based not only on urgency but on long-term value. These shifts do not require complex analytical frameworks; they require attention to how work fits within a larger system.

Throughout the chapters that follow, you will encounter familiar workplace situations—being assigned a task without context, prioritizing among competing demands, attending meetings where decisions are being shaped, or resolving recurring operational problems. These situations are intentionally ordinary. They represent the moments where most work actually happens and where the opportunity to think strategically often goes unnoticed.

Each chapter will explore how a small change in perspective during such moments can gradually transform the way you approach your role. The aim is not to replace execution excellence but to complement it with broader awareness. Reliable delivery remains essential; strategic thinking ensures that what is delivered contributes meaningfully to larger objectives.

You do not need to wait for a promotion to begin thinking strategically. You can start by asking slightly different questions about the work already on your desk. What larger outcome is this task meant to support? Who else might be affected by this decision? What consequences might unfold over time? Where does this work fit within the priorities of the organization?

When these questions become part of your daily thinking, work begins to look different. Tasks are no longer isolated activities; they become contributions to a broader flow of value creation. Decisions are no longer limited to immediate fixes; they are considered in light of future implications. Conversations are no longer limited to updates; they include insights that reflect awareness of context and impact.

This shift—from doing tasks to understanding their significance—is the essence of thinking beyond the task.

The chapters ahead invite you to practice this shift through real, relatable work situations. Rather than presenting abstract models of strategy, the book focuses on how strategic thinking can be cultivated through everyday experiences. By reflecting on how you interpret assignments, prioritize work, solve problems, and communicate ideas, you can gradually develop a mindset that is attentive not only to what needs to be done, but to why it matters and what it leads to.

Strategic thinking, then, is not an additional responsibility layered on top of your existing workload. It is a different way of engaging with the same work—one that connects effort to impact, action to consequence, and role to organizational purpose. When this way of thinking becomes habitual, even routine tasks can become opportunities to contribute with greater depth and foresight.

The journey begins with a simple but powerful question:
Are you only completing the task, or are you thinking beyond it?

# PART I

## Shifting How You See Your Work

Strategic thinking does not begin with sophisticated frameworks or complex analysis. It begins with a shift in how you see your everyday work. Many professionals assume that becoming more strategic requires new responsibilities, greater authority, or exposure to high-level planning discussions. In reality, the first transformation is far more fundamental: it is the movement from viewing work as a series of assigned tasks to seeing it as a set of contributions that create value within a larger system.

In most roles, tasks arrive with clear instructions, deadlines, and expected outputs. This clarity is useful and necessary. It helps ensure coordination, accountability, and timely execution. Over time, however, this mode of working can shape how individuals interpret their responsibilities. Work becomes defined primarily by what needs to be done next rather than by the broader purpose that the work is meant to serve. As long as tasks are completed efficiently, performance appears satisfactory, even if the deeper impact of those tasks remains unexplored.

Shifting toward strategic thinking requires expanding this lens. Instead of asking only, "What is the task?" one begins to ask, "What outcome is this task meant to influence?" This question may seem simple, yet it opens the door to a more thoughtful engagement with work. It invites consideration of context, priorities, dependencies, and future implications. Gradually, tasks stop appearing as isolated units of activity and start revealing their place within a larger chain of value creation.

This shift is especially important for employees who aspire to grow into broader leadership roles. Organizations often look for individuals who not only execute reliably but also demonstrate awareness of how their work connects to team goals, customer outcomes, and long-term organizational direction. Such awareness signals readiness for greater responsibility because it reflects the ability to think beyond immediate instructions and consider the wider consequences of decisions and actions.

The chapters in this part focus on foundational perspective shifts that enable this transformation. They do not introduce complex strategic tools. Instead, they explore how everyday interpretations of work—how you understand your role, your responsibilities, and your contribution—can either keep you confined to a task-oriented mindset or gradually expand your thinking toward value and impact.

The first shift involves moving from completing tasks to creating value. This requires recognizing that every assignment exists because it serves some larger objective, even if that objective is not always made explicit. When individuals begin to identify and align with that objective, their work naturally becomes more thoughtful and purposeful.

The second shift is about seeing the bigger picture of your role. Most positions are designed as parts of larger processes that span multiple teams and functions. Understanding how your work influences and is influenced by others enables better anticipation of needs, smoother coordination, and more informed decision-making. It also fosters a sense of ownership that goes beyond narrow role boundaries.

The third shift involves thinking beyond formal job descriptions. While clarity about responsibilities is important, rigid adherence to role definitions can sometimes limit initiative and perspective. Strategic thinking does not mean overstepping authority; it means remaining attentive to opportunities where your insight, coordination, or proactive communication can enhance overall outcomes without disrupting established structures.

Together, these shifts form the foundation of thinking beyond the task. They prepare you to approach everyday work with a broader perspective, making it possible to contribute not only through execution but also through awareness of context and impact. As these ways of seeing become more natural, strategic thinking gradually evolves from a deliberate effort into an intuitive habit that shapes how you interpret assignments, make decisions, and engage with colleagues.

The chapters that follow explore these shifts through common workplace situations—finishing assigned work, understanding how roles connect to larger goals, and navigating the boundaries of responsibility. By reflecting on these familiar experiences, you will begin to notice how small changes in perspective can significantly influence how your work is perceived and how effectively it contributes to organizational priorities.

Strategic thinking, therefore, does not begin with changing what you do. It begins with changing how you see what you already do.

# Chapter 1

## From Completing Tasks to Creating Value

In many workplaces, performance is often equated with task completion. If assignments are delivered on time, emails are responded to promptly, and instructions are followed accurately, an employee is generally seen as dependable and efficient. These qualities are important and form the foundation of professional credibility. However, as individuals progress in their careers, they often discover that consistent task completion, while necessary, is not always sufficient to be perceived as strategic or impactful.

This realization can be confusing. From the employee's perspective, they are doing exactly what is expected of them. They meet deadlines, produce outputs, and address immediate requirements. Yet feedback from managers may include phrases such as, "You need to think more strategically," or "Try to look at the bigger picture." Without clear guidance, such feedback can feel vague and difficult to translate into concrete action.

The distinction lies in the difference between completing tasks and creating value.

Completing a task means fulfilling the immediate requirement associated with an assignment. Creating value means understanding how that assignment contributes to a broader objective and shaping your approach so that the outcome meaningfully advances that objective. The task may remain the same, but the mindset with which it is approached changes the nature of the contribution.

Consider a simple example. An employee is asked to prepare a weekly report summarizing team performance. A task-focused approach would involve collecting the required data, formatting it according to established templates, and submitting it before the deadline. The work is completed correctly, and expectations are met. A value-focused approach, however, begins by asking a different question: "How will this report be used, and what decisions might it influence?"

With this perspective, the employee may highlight trends, flag emerging risks, or draw attention to patterns that require managerial attention. Instead of merely presenting data, the report becomes a tool for better decision-making. The task has not changed, but the value created has significantly increased.

This shift from task completion to value creation requires a subtle yet powerful change in how assignments are interpreted. Rather than viewing work as a checklist of activities to be executed, it becomes a set of opportunities to contribute to outcomes that extend beyond the immediate deliverable. Over time, individuals who consistently demonstrate this orientation are perceived not only as reliable executors but also as thoughtful contributors who understand the purpose behind their work.

One reason many professionals remain at the task level is that organizational systems often reinforce this mode of working. Deadlines emphasize speed, performance metrics track outputs, and managers frequently focus on whether deliverables have been completed. In such an environment, pausing to reflect on broader implications may feel like a luxury rather than a responsibility. As a result, individuals naturally optimize for efficiency in completing what has been asked, even if doing so limits their ability to contribute more strategically.

Another contributing factor is the absence of explicit context. Tasks are sometimes assigned without a detailed explanation of how they fit into larger goals or projects. When context is missing, employees may not feel empowered to question or explore the broader purpose of their work. They may assume that their role is simply to execute instructions accurately rather than to interpret and enhance the value of the output.

Developing a value-creation mindset begins with reclaiming that sense of context. It involves recognizing that every task exists because it serves some larger need, whether related to customer satisfaction, operational efficiency, risk management, or strategic planning. Even when this need is not fully articulated, it can often be inferred by considering who requested the work, how the output will be used, and what problems it is intended to address.

This way of thinking gradually changes how you engage with everyday assignments. When you receive a task, instead of immediately focusing only on how to complete it, you begin by reflecting on the outcome it is meant to support. This reflection does not require lengthy analysis; often, a few moments of consideration are sufficient to identify the broader purpose. Once this purpose becomes clear, decisions about prioritization, depth of analysis, and communication style can be aligned more closely with the value the task is expected to create.

Importantly, creating value does not mean expanding the scope of every assignment beyond what is reasonable or expected. It does not require taking on additional responsibilities without coordination or approval. Rather, it means ensuring that the work you already perform is thoughtfully shaped so that it meaningfully supports the larger objectives it is connected to. Sometimes, this may involve highlighting key insights, anticipating questions, or providing a concise interpretation of findings. At other times, it may simply involve clarifying assumptions to ensure that the output is aligned with the decision it is meant to inform.

Over time, this orientation influences how others perceive your contribution. Managers and colleagues begin to recognize that your work not only fulfils requirements but also advances understanding and supports better decision-making. You are seen as someone who thinks about impact, not just activity. This perception often leads to greater trust, more complex assignments, and increased involvement in discussions where direction and priorities are being shaped.

The movement from completing tasks to creating value is therefore not a dramatic transformation but a gradual evolution in perspective. It is cultivated through repeated attention to the purpose behind assignments and a consistent effort to align outputs with that purpose. As this mindset strengthens, everyday work begins to feel more meaningful because it is no longer experienced as a series of disconnected activities but as a set of contributions that influence real outcomes.

At its core, strategic thinking often begins with this simple awareness: the goal is not only to finish the task, but to ensure that the task meaningfully moves something forward.

**Practice Prompts: Thinking Beyond the Task**

- What larger outcome is this task meant to influence?

- Who will use the output of this work, and what decisions might depend on it?
- How can I present this work so that it highlights insights, not just information?
- If this task were done exceptionally well, what additional value could it create?
- At the end of today, can I describe the value I contributed, not just the tasks I completed?

*****

# Chapter 2

## Seeing the Bigger Picture of Your Role

Many professionals perform their roles with diligence and competence. They understand their responsibilities, meet expectations, and deliver consistent results. Yet, despite this reliability, they sometimes feel disconnected from the larger direction of the organization. Their work appears to exist within well-defined boundaries, and while those boundaries provide clarity, they can also limit perspective. The question that often remains unasked is: "How does my role fit into the larger system in which the organization operates?"

Strategic thinking begins to deepen when individuals start seeing their role not as an isolated set of duties but as a component of a broader network of activities that collectively create value. Every function, team, and individual contribution is connected, directly or indirectly, to organizational goals. When these connections remain invisible, work can feel fragmented. When they become visible, even routine tasks acquire greater significance and direction.

Consider an employee working in a support function such as operations, finance, human resources, or quality assurance. The daily responsibilities may revolve around processing requests, preparing documents, reviewing data, or ensuring compliance with established procedures.

Each of these tasks is important, but their true significance often lies in how they enable other teams to perform effectively, make informed decisions, or deliver better outcomes to customers. Without recognizing this linkage, the work may appear procedural rather than impactful.

Seeing the bigger picture involves understanding these interdependencies. It requires asking how your outputs become inputs for someone else's work and how delays, errors, or improvements in your area might ripple across the organization. This awareness gradually transforms the perception of responsibility. Instead of focusing only on completing assigned tasks accurately, individuals begin to consider how their work influences the efficiency, clarity, and effectiveness of others.

One common barrier to developing this perspective is the natural tendency to remain within clearly defined role boundaries. Job descriptions, performance metrics, and reporting structures reinforce the idea that each person is accountable primarily for their own domain. While this clarity prevents confusion and overlap, it can also unintentionally discourage curiosity about how different parts of the organization connect. Employees may assume that understanding the larger system is the responsibility of managers, not of those executing specific functions.

However, strategic thinking does not require control over the entire system. It requires awareness of how one's work fits within it. This awareness can develop gradually through observation, conversation, and reflection. By paying attention to how information flows across teams, how decisions are made, and how different functions depend on each other, individuals begin to map the context in which their role operates. Over time, this mental map becomes a valuable guide for making more thoughtful decisions and anticipating potential challenges.

For example, imagine a project coordinator responsible for compiling updates from multiple departments. A narrow view of the role would involve collecting inputs, consolidating them into a report, and forwarding the document to senior management. A broader perspective would involve recognizing patterns across departments, identifying areas where timelines might clash, or noting dependencies that could affect overall project progress. By sharing these observations, the coordinator moves from being a transmitter of information to a contributor of insight.

This shift is not about assuming responsibilities that belong to others. It is about becoming more attentive to context so that your work aligns more closely with organizational priorities. When individuals understand the broader goals their team is pursuing, they are better able to judge which aspects of their work require greater emphasis, where proactive communication might prevent misunderstandings, and how to adapt their approach when circumstances change.

Another important aspect of seeing the bigger picture is recognizing that organizational goals often involve trade-offs between competing priorities. A decision that benefits one team might create constraints for another. When employees understand these dynamics, they are more likely to approach issues with balanced judgment rather than advocating solely from the perspective of their immediate function. This balanced approach signals maturity in thinking and builds credibility in cross-functional interactions.

Developing this perspective also enhances collaboration. When individuals appreciate how their work influences others, they communicate more thoughtfully, provide clearer inputs, and anticipate the information needs of colleagues in other areas. Meetings become more meaningful because discussions move beyond narrow updates to include consideration of shared objectives and coordinated action. Over time, this fosters a sense of collective ownership for outcomes rather than fragmented responsibility for isolated tasks.

Importantly, seeing the bigger picture does not require perfect knowledge of the entire organization. It begins with small steps:

understanding your team's key objectives, learning how your outputs are used downstream, and observing how decisions in one area affect work in another. Each insight expands your mental model of the organization, enabling you to interpret situations more strategically.

As this awareness grows, your role begins to feel less confined and more connected. You are no longer simply executing assigned duties; you are participating in a larger process of value creation. Decisions about how to prioritize tasks, how much detail to include in communication, or when to escalate concerns become easier because they are guided by an understanding of broader impact rather than limited to immediate requirements.

Ultimately, seeing the bigger picture of your role is about shifting from a position-centered view of work to a system-centered view. It is about recognizing that every role, regardless of level, contributes to outcomes that extend beyond its immediate scope. When this perspective becomes habitual, everyday actions are informed by an awareness of how they influence the larger whole, and strategic thinking begins to emerge naturally from routine work.

**Practice Prompts: Thinking Beyond the Task**

- How does the work I do enable other teams or functions to perform effectively?
- Who depends on the output of my role, and how might delays or errors affect them?
- What are the key goals my team is trying to achieve, and how does my work support them?
- When I make decisions in my role, what broader impact might they have on related processes or stakeholders?
- What one step can I take this week to better understand how different parts of the organization connect?

# Chapter 3

## Thinking Beyond Your Job Description

In many organizations, job descriptions provide clarity about roles and responsibilities. They define what is expected, establish accountability, and help ensure that work is distributed efficiently. This clarity is valuable, especially in complex environments where coordination across multiple functions is necessary. Yet, over time, strict reliance on job descriptions can also create an unintended limitation: individuals may begin to see their role only in terms of what is explicitly listed, rather than in terms of the broader contribution they are capable of making.

This limitation often appears in subtle ways. When new issues arise that fall slightly outside defined responsibilities, the instinctive response may be, "This is not part of my role." While such a response protects boundaries and prevents role confusion, it can also restrict initiative and perspective. Strategic thinking requires a more nuanced approach—one that respects role clarity while remaining attentive to opportunities where thoughtful involvement can enhance overall outcomes.

Thinking beyond your job description does not mean disregarding established responsibilities or assuming authority that has not been granted. Instead, it involves recognizing that organizational work rarely fits perfectly within neatly defined boxes. Real-world situations often span multiple roles, require cross-functional understanding, and benefit from proactive coordination. In such moments, the ability to look beyond formal boundaries and consider the larger objective becomes an important aspect of strategic thinking.

Consider a scenario where a team member notices a recurring issue affecting project timelines. The problem may originate in another department, and technically, resolving it may not fall within their formal responsibility. A strictly role-bound approach would involve completing one's own tasks and leaving the issue to be addressed elsewhere. A broader, more strategic approach might involve raising the observation constructively, sharing relevant data, or initiating a conversation that brings the right stakeholders together to address the root cause. The individual is not overstepping authority but contributing to a more effective overall outcome.

One reason employees hesitate to think beyond their job description is the concern that doing so may be perceived as interference or overreach. This concern is understandable, particularly in hierarchical environments where roles and reporting lines are clearly defined. However, strategic contribution is less about taking control and more about offering perspective. When communicated with respect and clarity, such perspective is often welcomed because it helps prevent issues, improve coordination, and align efforts toward shared goals.

Another barrier is the belief that only those in formal leadership positions are expected to think about broader implications. Employees may assume that their role is to execute instructions while managers handle the larger picture. While leadership roles do carry broader responsibility, organizations increasingly value individuals at all levels who demonstrate awareness of context and who proactively highlight potential risks, dependencies, or opportunities. Such behavior signals readiness for greater responsibility because it reflects the ability to engage with complexity rather than operate only within narrow task boundaries.

Developing this capability begins with a shift in how responsibilities are interpreted. Instead of viewing the job description as a rigid boundary, it can be seen as a core area of accountability within a larger ecosystem of work. The question then becomes: "Within my area of responsibility, what additional awareness or coordination could enhance the effectiveness of the overall process?" This question encourages thoughtful initiative without disregarding role clarity.

For example, a customer support executive may notice recurring patterns in client feedback that indicate a product usability issue. Addressing product design may not be part of the executive's formal role. However, systematically documenting these patterns and sharing them with the product team provides valuable insight that can improve long-term customer experience. The individual remains within their domain of responsibility while contributing strategically to organizational learning.

Thinking beyond your job description also involves recognizing when restraint is appropriate. Strategic thinking is not about intervening in every issue or assuming that one must solve problems across all functions. It is about exercising judgment—knowing when to contribute perspective, when to collaborate, and when to focus deeply on one's own responsibilities. This balance preserves clarity while enabling meaningful contribution beyond narrow task execution.

Over time, individuals who demonstrate this balanced initiative are often seen as collaborative and forward-thinking. They are trusted to handle more complex assignments because they show an ability to consider implications that extend beyond immediate deliverables. Their input becomes valued not only for its technical accuracy but also for its relevance to broader organizational priorities.

This evolution does not happen suddenly. It emerges through repeated small actions: asking clarifying questions about how work fits into larger processes, sharing observations that could prevent future issues, and remaining attentive to how decisions in one area might influence outcomes in another. Each of these actions signals a mindset that looks beyond formal definitions toward meaningful contribution.

Ultimately, thinking beyond your job description is about aligning your efforts with the purpose behind your role rather than being confined by its wording. Job descriptions define what you are accountable for; strategic thinking invites you to consider how your awareness, initiative, and coordination can enhance the value of that accountability. When approached with respect for organizational structures and sensitivity to collaboration, this mindset enables you to contribute in ways that extend beyond task execution while remaining grounded in your core responsibilities.

**Practice Prompts: Thinking Beyond the Task**

- Where in my work do I see issues or opportunities that extend beyond my immediate responsibilities?
- How can I share relevant observations constructively without overstepping authority?
- When does stepping back and staying within my role create clarity, and when might proactive coordination add value?

- How does my role connect with the work of other teams, and where could better collaboration improve outcomes?
- This week, what is one small initiative I can take that supports the larger objective while respecting role boundaries?

# PART II

## Everyday Moments That Require Strategic Thinking

Strategic thinking is often imagined as an activity reserved for major decisions, long-term planning sessions, or senior leadership discussions. In reality, it emerges far more frequently in ordinary moments of daily work. These moments may appear routine—prioritizing tasks, responding to unexpected issues, participating in meetings, or deciding how deeply to analyze a problem. Yet each of these situations carries implicit choices about focus, trade-offs, and consequences. The way these choices are interpreted and acted upon gradually shapes whether an individual remains primarily task-oriented or develops a more strategic orientation.

In day-to-day work, individuals rarely encounter clearly labeled "strategic" decisions. Instead, they face practical questions: Which task should be addressed first? How much context is needed before responding to an issue? Should a potential risk be highlighted now or observed further? Is it better to resolve a problem quickly or invest time in understanding its root cause? These questions do not initially appear strategic, yet they involve judgments about priorities, implications, and long-term impact. Over time, consistent attention to such judgments builds the habit of thinking beyond immediate execution.

One of the reasons strategic thinking feels elusive is that it is often associated with scale. Employees may assume that unless they are making decisions affecting large budgets or organizational direction, their role does not involve strategic thinking. This assumption overlooks the cumulative effect of everyday decisions. Small choices about how to allocate time, what information to emphasize, when to escalate concerns, or how to frame a recommendation can influence outcomes far more than isolated high-level decisions. Strategic thinking, therefore, is less about occasional grand decisions and more about the quality of judgment applied in frequent, routine situations.

Another challenge arises from the pace of modern work environments. Continuous deadlines and rapid communication cycles encourage quick responses and immediate problem-solving. While speed is valuable, it can also reduce opportunities for reflection. Individuals may move from one task to another without pausing to consider broader implications or alternative approaches. Over time, this reinforces a reactive mode of working in which efficiency is prioritized but foresight remains underdeveloped.

Developing strategic thinking in everyday moments requires inserting small pauses of awareness into this fast-paced flow of work. These pauses are not meant to slow productivity but to enhance judgment. They involve briefly considering questions such as: What is the larger objective behind this request? Which option aligns best with long-term priorities? How might this decision affect related teams or future work? Even a short reflection can shift the response from purely reactive to more thoughtful and context-aware.

The chapters in this part explore common workplace situations where such reflection can be particularly valuable. These situations include being given a problem rather than a clearly defined task, managing competing priorities when everything appears urgent, anticipating consequences before taking action, and contributing meaningfully in meetings where decisions are being shaped. Each scenario represents a frequent point of choice where individuals can either focus narrowly on immediate execution or adopt a broader perspective that considers context, trade-offs, and future implications.

Approaching these moments strategically does not require formal authority or access to privileged information. It requires attentiveness to how decisions are framed and a willingness to think a step beyond the immediate requirement. For example, when presented with a problem, the instinctive reaction may be to implement the quickest available fix. A more strategic response would involve asking whether the issue is symptomatic of a deeper pattern and whether addressing root causes could prevent recurrence. Similarly, when faced with multiple urgent requests, the immediate tendency may be to respond to the most visible demand, whereas a strategic approach would involve assessing which task contributes most significantly to key objectives or long-term value.

These distinctions are subtle but meaningful. They reflect not a difference in intelligence or capability but a difference in orientation—whether work is approached primarily as a sequence of tasks to be completed or as a series of decisions that influence broader outcomes. Over time, individuals who consistently apply this broader orientation begin to be recognized as thoughtful contributors who understand not only what needs to be done but also why it matters and how it connects to larger goals.

It is important to note that strategic thinking in everyday moments does not imply overanalyzing every decision or delaying action in pursuit of perfect clarity. Practical work often requires timely responses and pragmatic judgment. The aim is not to replace action with analysis but to enrich action with awareness. A brief consideration of context, consequences, and priorities can significantly improve the quality of decisions without compromising efficiency.

As you engage with the chapters in this part, you will be invited to reflect on familiar situations that occur regularly in your work. By examining how you typically respond to these situations and how a slight shift in perspective could alter the outcome, you will begin to develop a more intuitive sense of when and how to apply strategic thinking. Over time, these small adjustments accumulate, gradually transforming routine decisions into opportunities for broader contribution and deeper impact.

Strategic thinking, therefore, is not a separate activity added to your workload. It is a way of engaging more thoughtfully with the decisions you already make every day.

# Chapter 4

## When You Are Given a Problem, Not Just a Task

In many workplace situations, individuals are not given clearly defined tasks with step-by-step instructions. Instead, they are presented with problems: an issue has emerged, a process is not working as expected, or a result is not aligning with desired outcomes. The request may simply be, "Please look into this," or "Can you resolve this issue?" At first glance, such situations may appear similar to routine assignments, yet they require a different kind of thinking. They demand interpretation, judgment, and a deeper understanding of context.

A task typically has a clear scope and expected output. A problem, on the other hand, is open-ended. It involves ambiguity about causes, potential consequences, and the most appropriate course of action. When individuals approach a problem with a purely task-oriented mindset, they may focus on implementing the quickest visible fix. While this may provide immediate relief, it does not always address underlying causes. As a result, the same issue may recur, consuming time and energy repeatedly without leading to lasting improvement.

Strategic thinking begins to emerge when a problem is interpreted not merely as something to be solved quickly, but as something to be understood more deeply. The first step in this shift is to ask: "What is actually causing this issue?" rather than only, "How can I fix this right now?" This question opens the possibility of exploring patterns, dependencies, and systemic factors that may be contributing to the problem. It encourages a move from reactive correction to thoughtful diagnosis.

Consider a scenario where a recurring delay is observed in delivering project updates. A task-focused response might involve reminding team members to submit their inputs on time or working extra hours to compile missing information. These actions may temporarily reduce delays, but they do not necessarily explain why the delays occur repeatedly. A more strategic approach would involve examining whether timelines are realistic, whether dependencies across teams are clearly defined, or whether communication channels are causing confusion about expectations. By identifying and addressing root causes, the individual contributes not only to solving the immediate problem but also to preventing similar issues in the future.

Another aspect of approaching problems strategically is recognizing that different solutions may have different implications. Some fixes may resolve the visible symptom but create additional complexity elsewhere. Others may require slightly more effort initially but lead to smoother operations over time. Evaluating these trade-offs requires stepping back from the urgency of the moment and considering the broader impact of each option. Even a brief reflection on such implications can significantly improve the quality of decisions.

In many organizations, the pressure to respond quickly can discourage deeper examination of problems. Speed is often valued because it signals responsiveness and ownership. However, when speed becomes the only priority, it can lead to repetitive cycles of correction without meaningful learning. Strategic thinking does not reject the importance of timely action; instead, it balances responsiveness with thoughtful analysis. The aim is to act efficiently while ensuring that actions are informed by an understanding of underlying dynamics.

When presented with a problem, another useful perspective is to consider who else might be affected by both the issue and its resolution. Problems rarely exist in isolation. They often influence multiple stakeholders, processes, or outcomes. By mapping these connections, individuals can anticipate potential ripple effects of different solutions and choose approaches that align with broader objectives rather than addressing only a narrow aspect of the situation.

Communication also plays a significant role in handling problems strategically. Instead of reporting only that an issue has been resolved, individuals can share insights about what caused the issue and what measures could prevent recurrence. This transforms the interaction from a simple status update to a learning opportunity for the team or organization. Over time, such communication builds a reputation for thoughtful problem-solving rather than quick but temporary fixes.

It is important to recognize that not every problem requires extensive analysis. Some issues are straightforward and can be addressed efficiently with established solutions. The key is to develop the judgment to distinguish between routine problems and those that indicate deeper patterns or potential future risks. This judgment improves with experience and reflection, especially when individuals review past situations to understand which problems were one-time events and which were symptoms of larger systemic issues.

Approaching problems strategically also fosters a sense of ownership that extends beyond immediate resolution. When individuals take the time to understand why something went wrong and how similar issues can be prevented, they contribute to organizational learning and improvement. This mindset signals maturity in thinking and often leads to greater trust from colleagues and managers, who come to rely on such individuals not only for execution but also for thoughtful insight.

Ultimately, being given a problem rather than a task is an invitation to think beyond immediate correction. It offers an opportunity to exercise judgment, understand context, and contribute to more sustainable solutions. By viewing problems as chances to learn about underlying processes and interdependencies, individuals gradually shift from reactive execution to proactive and strategic engagement with their work.

**Practice Prompts: Thinking Beyond the Task**

- What might be the underlying causes of this problem, beyond the immediate symptom?
- If I implement the quickest fix, will the issue likely recur in the future?
- Who else could be affected by this problem and by the solution I choose?
- What additional information would help me understand the broader context of this issue?
- After resolving the problem, what can I document or share to help prevent similar issues later?

# Chapter 5

## Prioritizing When Everything Feels Urgent

One of the most common challenges in everyday work is the feeling that everything requires immediate attention. Emails arrive continuously, meetings are scheduled back-to-back, deadlines overlap, and multiple stakeholders expect prompt responses. In such situations, individuals often move rapidly from one task to another, attempting to address each demand as quickly as possible. While this approach reflects diligence and responsiveness, it can also lead to a reactive pattern of working in which urgency, rather than importance, determines what receives attention.

Prioritization is frequently viewed as a time-management skill, yet it is fundamentally a strategic thinking capability. It requires judging which actions will create the most meaningful impact over time, not merely which tasks appear most pressing in the moment. When everything seems urgent, the challenge is not simply to work faster but to think more carefully about what truly deserves priority.

A purely task-focused approach to prioritization often relies on visible signals such as deadlines, reminders, or repeated follow-ups from stakeholders. Tasks that generate the most immediate pressure are addressed first, while those with longer-term implications may be postponed. Although this method reduces short-term tension, it can gradually shift attention away from work that contributes significantly to long-term objectives. Over time, individuals may find themselves consistently busy yet unsure whether their efforts are advancing the most important goals.

Strategic prioritization begins with a different question: "Which of these tasks contributes most meaningfully to desired outcomes?" This question invites a shift from urgency-driven action to value-oriented judgment. It encourages individuals to consider not only when a task is due but also how it aligns with key priorities, how it influences future work, and what consequences might arise if it is delayed.

For example, imagine an employee managing three simultaneous requests: responding to routine informational queries, preparing a detailed analysis for an upcoming decision, and addressing a minor operational issue that has generated several reminders. A purely urgency-based approach might lead to addressing the operational issue first because it is receiving the most visible attention. A strategic approach would involve recognizing that the analysis will inform an important decision affecting multiple teams and that delaying it could have broader implications. The employee might then allocate focused time to the analysis while communicating transparently about timelines for the other tasks. The visible urgency is acknowledged, but the underlying importance guides the prioritization.

Another dimension of strategic prioritization involves understanding that not all urgent tasks carry equal long-term impact. Some urgent matters are genuinely critical and require immediate action to prevent significant disruption. Others appear urgent primarily because they are highly visible or because they address short-term concerns rather than enduring outcomes. Distinguishing between these categories requires attentiveness to context and an awareness of organizational priorities.

This distinction is particularly relevant in collaborative environments where multiple stakeholders have competing expectations. Each stakeholder naturally views their request as important, and their sense of urgency may be genuine from their perspective. Strategic prioritization does not dismiss these concerns; instead, it integrates them within a broader assessment of overall objectives. By communicating clearly about how tasks are being sequenced and why certain items are being addressed first, individuals can maintain trust while ensuring that their effort is directed toward the most impactful work.

The challenge of prioritization is compounded when individuals attempt to respond to every request immediately, believing that doing so demonstrates commitment and reliability. While responsiveness is valuable, constant immediate action can fragment attention and reduce the quality of thinking applied to complex tasks. Strategic thinking often requires uninterrupted time to reflect, analyze, and anticipate implications. Without consciously protecting such time, important work may be repeatedly interrupted by less consequential but more visible demands.

Developing a strategic approach to prioritization therefore involves not only selecting which tasks to address first but also deciding how to structure time and attention. This may include setting aside dedicated periods for high-impact work, grouping similar routine tasks together, and establishing realistic expectations with stakeholders about response timelines. Such practices signal that prioritization is being managed thoughtfully rather than reactively.

Another useful perspective is to consider the future consequences of today's choices. When a task with long-term significance is consistently postponed in favor of immediate demands, its eventual urgency may increase dramatically, creating avoidable pressure later. Conversely, investing time early in high-impact work can reduce future complexity and prevent crises. This forward-looking view aligns daily decisions with longer-term outcomes and reinforces the habit of thinking beyond the present moment.

Over time, individuals who prioritize strategically are perceived as more composed and deliberate in their work. They are less likely to be overwhelmed by fluctuating demands because their decisions are guided by clear principles rather than by immediate pressure alone. Colleagues and managers come to rely on their judgment, recognizing that they focus effort where it will produce the greatest value rather than simply where noise or urgency is highest.

Ultimately, prioritizing when everything feels urgent is about moving from reactive responsiveness to thoughtful judgment. It requires acknowledging immediate demands while also considering their relative importance, long-term impact, and alignment with broader goals. By consistently applying this lens, everyday decisions about where to direct attention become opportunities to practice strategic thinking and to ensure that effort contributes meaningfully to outcomes that matter most.

**Practice Prompts: Thinking Beyond the Task**

- Which of today's tasks will have the most significant impact one month from now?
- Am I prioritizing based on urgency signals or on alignment with key goals?
- What might happen if I delay this task—today, this week, or this month?

- Which task, if done thoughtfully now, could prevent greater work or problems later?
- How can I communicate my priorities clearly so others understand the reasoning behind my sequencing decisions?

# Chapter 6

## Anticipating Consequences Before Acting

In the flow of everyday work, decisions are often made quickly. Requests arrive, issues surface, and actions are taken in rapid succession to maintain momentum and meet expectations. This responsiveness is valuable and often necessary. However, when actions are guided only by immediate requirements, their broader implications may remain unexamined. Strategic thinking begins to deepen when individuals pause briefly to consider not only what needs to be done now, but also what effects their actions might create over time.

Anticipating consequences does not require predicting every possible outcome. It involves developing the habit of asking how today's decisions might influence future work, relationships, and priorities. Even small choices—how information is communicated, how a problem is resolved, or how a decision is framed—can set patterns that shape future expectations and behaviors. By reflecting on these patterns, individuals move from reactive action to more thoughtful engagement with their responsibilities.

Consider a situation where a team member consistently responds to last-minute requests by adjusting their schedule and accommodating the changes without discussion. While this flexibility demonstrates commitment, it may gradually signal that such requests can always be accommodated without impact. Over time, this can lead to an increase in last-minute demands, creating ongoing pressure and reducing the ability to focus on planned priorities. Anticipating this consequence allows the individual to respond differently—perhaps by fulfilling the request while also clarifying timelines or discussing how earlier notice could improve quality and efficiency in the future.

This example illustrates how immediate actions can shape longer-term patterns. Strategic thinking involves recognizing that each response contributes to an evolving system of expectations and norms. When individuals act without considering these evolving effects, they may unintentionally reinforce behaviors that make future work more difficult. When they act with awareness of potential consequences, they can influence those patterns in more constructive ways.

Another area where anticipating consequences is valuable is in decision-making under uncertainty. Often, individuals must choose a course of action without having complete information. In such cases, the instinct may be to select the option that resolves the most visible issue quickly. A more strategic approach involves considering how each option might unfold over time. Which choice is likely to reduce complexity in the long run? Which might create dependencies or require additional adjustments later? By reflecting on these questions, individuals can make decisions that balance immediate needs with future stability.

Anticipating consequences also requires understanding that different stakeholders may experience the effects of decisions in different ways. An action that simplifies work for one team might increase workload for another. A change that improves short-term efficiency might introduce risks if not carefully implemented. Strategic thinking involves looking beyond one's immediate context to consider how others might be affected and how their responses could influence subsequent outcomes.

Communication plays a crucial role in this process. When individuals explain not only what they are doing but also why they are taking a particular approach and what outcomes they anticipate, they invite broader understanding and alignment. Such communication reduces misunderstandings and allows others to provide input that may refine the decision further. In this way, anticipating consequences becomes a collaborative rather than solitary activity.

It is important to note that anticipating consequences does not mean overanalyzing every action or delaying decisions unnecessarily. In fast-paced environments, excessive deliberation can hinder progress. The aim is to develop a balanced approach: acting decisively while maintaining awareness of likely implications. Often, a brief moment of reflection is sufficient to surface key considerations that would otherwise be overlooked.

Developing this habit becomes easier with experience, especially when individuals take time to review past situations. Reflecting on how earlier decisions influenced later outcomes provides valuable insight into patterns and recurring dynamics. Over time, such reflection sharpens judgment and makes anticipation more intuitive, enabling quicker yet still thoughtful responses.

As this mindset strengthens, individuals begin to see their actions not as isolated responses but as contributions to an ongoing sequence of events. They recognize that each decision influences the context in which future decisions will be made. This awareness encourages a more deliberate approach to everyday work, one that aligns immediate actions with longer-term intentions and organizational priorities.

Ultimately, anticipating consequences before acting is about extending one's thinking slightly beyond the present moment. It involves recognizing that every decision has a trajectory, shaping what becomes easier or more difficult in the future. By consistently considering these trajectories, individuals develop a strategic orientation that informs not only what they do but also how their actions influence the evolving landscape of work around them.

**Practice Prompts: Thinking Beyond the Task**

- If I take this action now, what outcomes might it create over the next few weeks or months?
- How might this decision shape future expectations about similar situations?
- Who else could be affected by this action, directly or indirectly?
- Is there an alternative approach that might require slightly more effort now but reduce future complexity?
- After completing this task, what patterns or consequences should I observe to learn for next time?

# Chapter 7

## Asking Better Questions in Meetings

Meetings are among the most common workplace experiences. They are where updates are shared, decisions are shaped, priorities are clarified, and problems are discussed. Yet for many employees, meetings are primarily spaces for listening and reporting rather than for contributing strategically. Individuals may provide status updates, respond to direct questions, or take notes, but hesitate to offer perspectives unless explicitly invited.

Strategic thinking often becomes visible in meetings not through long speeches or complex analyses, but through thoughtful questions. The quality of the questions asked can significantly influence the direction of a discussion. While statements provide information, questions open possibilities. They signal awareness of context, implications, and connections that may not yet have been fully considered.

In task-focused participation, an individual might limit contributions to reporting progress: "The report has been completed," or "The issue has been resolved." These updates are necessary, but they do not necessarily shape decision-making. A more strategic contribution might involve asking, "How will this change affect our timeline for the next phase?" or "What risks should we anticipate if we proceed with this approach?" Such questions demonstrate attention to broader implications and invite the group to think beyond immediate tasks.

One reason individuals hesitate to ask such questions is uncertainty about whether it is appropriate to challenge or expand the discussion. In hierarchical environments, employees may fear that asking broader questions could be interpreted as criticism or overstepping. However, when framed respectfully and with genuine curiosity, well-considered questions are often welcomed because they enhance collective understanding and improve decision quality.

Strategic questions tend to fall into several categories. Some focus on alignment: "How does this initiative support our larger objective?" Others address consequences: "What might be the long-term impact of this decision?" Still others explore interdependencies: "How will this affect other teams or stakeholders?" Each type of question broadens the conversation and encourages participants to consider dimensions that may not have been explicitly discussed.

For example, during a planning meeting, a team might agree on an aggressive timeline for launching a new initiative. A task-focused contribution would involve confirming deliverables and deadlines. A strategic question might be, "Do we have the necessary resources in place to sustain this pace without affecting ongoing commitments?" This inquiry does not oppose the plan but ensures that the decision is evaluated in light of capacity and trade-offs.

Another common scenario involves meetings where recurring issues are discussed repeatedly without clear resolution. Instead of participating passively, an individual might ask, “Are we addressing the underlying cause of this issue, or are we managing the symptoms?” This question gently redirects attention toward root causes and long-term solutions. Over time, such interventions help elevate the quality of dialogue within teams.

Asking better questions also enhances personal credibility. When colleagues observe that your contributions consistently prompt deeper reflection or clarify implications, they begin to associate you with thoughtful analysis rather than mere execution. This perception often leads to increased trust and inclusion in discussions where direction and priorities are being shaped.

Importantly, asking strategic questions requires preparation. Reviewing meeting agendas in advance, reflecting on how topics connect to broader goals, and anticipating potential risks or dependencies can equip you to contribute meaningfully. Preparation transforms meetings from passive listening sessions into opportunities for active engagement with organizational direction.

The tone and framing of questions matter as well. Questions should be posed with curiosity rather than confrontation. Phrasing such as "Can we explore..." or "How might this affect..." invites collaboration rather than defensiveness. The aim is not to challenge authority but to enrich understanding and strengthen decisions.

Over time, cultivating the habit of asking thoughtful questions influences how you experience meetings. Instead of viewing them as interruptions or routine obligations, you begin to see them as platforms for shaping outcomes. Each meeting becomes an opportunity to practice thinking beyond the immediate agenda and to consider how decisions connect to broader objectives.

Strategic thinking in meetings is therefore less about dominating conversations and more about elevating them. By consistently introducing questions that explore alignment, consequences, and interdependencies, you contribute to more informed and balanced decisions. These contributions, though subtle, gradually position you as someone who sees beyond tasks and engages with the larger picture.

Ultimately, asking better questions is one of the simplest and most powerful ways to practice strategic thinking in everyday work. It requires attentiveness, preparation, and courage, but it does not require formal authority. Through well-framed questions, you can influence how discussions unfold and how decisions are shaped—demonstrating that strategic thinking is as much about perspective as it is about position.

**Practice Prompts: Thinking Beyond the Task**

- In the next meeting I attend, what broader question can I prepare in advance?
- How does the topic of this meeting connect to larger team or organizational goals?
- What risks, trade-offs, or dependencies might not yet have been discussed?
- How can I frame my question in a way that invites reflection rather than defensiveness?
- After the meeting, did my contributions help clarify direction or deepen understanding?

# PART III

## Expanding Perspective from Self to System

Up to this point, we have explored how strategic thinking begins with shifts in everyday interpretation—moving from completing tasks to creating value, from reacting quickly to anticipating consequences, and from reporting updates to asking better questions. These shifts strengthen individual judgment and broaden personal perspective. The next stage of development involves expanding that perspective further—from focusing primarily on one's own role to understanding the larger system in which that role operates.

Every organization functions as a network of interdependent activities. Decisions in one area influence outcomes in another. Priorities shift in response to market conditions, resource constraints, and evolving goals. When individuals view their work only through the lens of personal responsibilities, they may miss these connections. As a result, actions that appear effective locally may create unintended challenges elsewhere. Strategic thinking deepens when individuals recognize these interdependencies and begin to evaluate decisions in light of system-wide impact.

Expanding from self to system does not require detailed knowledge of every function within the organization. It requires cultivating curiosity about how different pieces fit together. How do various teams coordinate to achieve shared objectives? Where do handoffs occur, and how might they create friction or delays? What assumptions guide decision-making across departments? By exploring these questions, individuals gradually develop a more integrated understanding of the organization's dynamics.

This systems-oriented perspective transforms the way problems, priorities, and initiatives are interpreted. For example, a delay in one team's output may initially appear as a localized inefficiency. Viewed through a broader lens, it may reflect capacity imbalances, unclear communication channels, or misaligned incentives across teams. Recognizing these possibilities encourages solutions that address underlying structures rather than isolated symptoms.

Another dimension of expanding perspective involves understanding trade-offs. Organizations rarely have unlimited resources or time. Choices must be made between competing initiatives, quality and speed, short-term gains and long-term investments. When individuals appreciate these trade-offs, they are better equipped to align their efforts with strategic priorities. They become more thoughtful in evaluating requests, recommending solutions, and allocating attention.

This shift also enhances collaboration. When employees recognize that others are navigating similar constraints and trade-offs, interactions become more empathetic and solution-oriented. Instead of advocating narrowly for their own team's objectives, individuals consider how proposals will influence broader outcomes. This balanced approach strengthens trust and supports more cohesive decision-making across functions.

Importantly, expanding from self to system does not diminish personal accountability. On the contrary, it strengthens it. When individuals understand how their work influences others, they become more attentive to quality, clarity, and timing. They recognize that their actions are part of a larger chain of value creation and that small adjustments in their approach can reduce friction or enhance coordination across the organization.

The chapters in this part focus on practical ways to develop this systems-oriented mindset. You will explore how to recognize interdependencies across functions, how to think in terms of trade-offs rather than isolated gains, and how to move from repeatedly solving surface problems to addressing deeper structural patterns. Each of these capabilities builds upon the earlier shifts discussed in the book, gradually reinforcing a more comprehensive and strategic approach to everyday work.

As your perspective expands, your contribution evolves. You are no longer simply managing your tasks effectively; you are engaging thoughtfully with the larger context in which those tasks exist. Decisions become informed by awareness of broader impact, and collaboration becomes guided by shared objectives rather than isolated priorities. Over time, this systemic understanding distinguishes individuals who are seen not only as reliable performers but as contributors who grasp the interconnected nature of organizational success.

Strategic thinking, at its core, is about seeing patterns and connections that extend beyond immediate boundaries. By expanding your perspective from self to system, you deepen your ability to make decisions that create value not just locally, but across the broader landscape of work.

# Chapter 8

## Understanding How Different Functions Connect

In most organizations, work is divided into functions—sales, marketing, operations, finance, technology, human resources, and others. Each function has its own objectives, expertise, and performance metrics. This specialization enables efficiency and clarity. However, it can also create silos where teams focus primarily on their own targets without fully appreciating how their work influences or depends upon others.

Strategic thinking strengthens significantly when individuals begin to understand how these different functions connect. Instead of viewing their role as an isolated unit of performance, they start to see it as one part of a larger, interconnected system. This shift transforms how problems are interpreted, how decisions are evaluated, and how collaboration is approached.

Consider a product launch initiative. The marketing team may focus on campaign visibility and customer engagement. The operations team may prioritize supply readiness and distribution efficiency. Finance may concentrate on cost control and margin projections. Technology may ensure platform stability and integration. Each team is pursuing legitimate and necessary goals. However, if these goals are pursued without understanding their interdependence, misalignment can occur. A marketing campaign may generate demand before operations is prepared to fulfill it. Cost controls may limit investment needed to sustain long-term growth. Technical constraints may delay commitments made externally.

When individuals within each function understand how their work affects others, they are more likely to anticipate potential friction and coordinate proactively. A marketing professional who understands operational constraints may adjust timelines or communicate capacity expectations clearly. An operations manager who recognizes revenue targets may prioritize certain deliveries to support critical accounts. Such awareness reduces conflict and strengthens collective effectiveness.

One way to cultivate this understanding is to examine the flow of work across functions. Ask yourself: Where does my output go next? Who relies on it? What information or resources do I receive from others to perform my role? Mapping these flows, even informally, reveals the dependencies that shape outcomes. It also highlights opportunities where clearer communication or improved coordination could enhance efficiency.

Another important aspect of cross-functional awareness is recognizing differing perspectives. Each function interprets priorities through its own lens. Sales may emphasize speed and customer responsiveness. Finance may focus on cost discipline and risk management. Operations may value consistency and process reliability. When individuals understand these differing lenses, they are less likely to interpret disagreements as personal or adversarial. Instead, they see them as reflections of legitimate but distinct priorities.

Strategic thinking involves integrating these perspectives rather than favoring one exclusively. For example, when evaluating a proposal that increases short-term revenue but raises operational complexity, a strategically minded individual considers both revenue potential and sustainability. They seek solutions that balance growth with operational feasibility rather than advocating solely from their functional standpoint.

This integrative approach also improves communication. When presenting ideas or recommendations, individuals who understand cross-functional implications can frame their message in ways that address the concerns of different stakeholders. They anticipate questions and highlight how the proposal supports broader objectives, not just their own function's goals. This increases credibility and facilitates smoother decision-making.

Developing cross-functional awareness does not require formal rotation across departments, though such experiences can be valuable. It begins with curiosity and dialogue. Participating actively in cross-team meetings, seeking clarification about how others' work connects to yours, and reflecting on how decisions in one area influence outcomes elsewhere all contribute to a more systemic understanding.

Over time, this broader perspective changes how you evaluate success. Instead of measuring performance solely by how well your immediate tasks are executed, you begin to assess how effectively your work contributes to coordinated outcomes across the organization. This shift signals maturity in thinking and often distinguishes individuals who are ready for expanded leadership responsibilities.

Ultimately, understanding how different functions connect transforms isolated efforts into coordinated contributions. It reduces unnecessary friction, enhances collaboration, and aligns actions with shared goals. Strategic thinking thrives in this interconnected view, where decisions are informed not only by local priorities but also by an awareness of how those decisions influence the broader organizational ecosystem.

**Practice Prompts: Thinking Beyond the Task**

- Who depends on the outputs of my function, and what challenges do they face?

- How might a change in my team's priorities affect other departments?
- What assumptions guide decision-making in other functions, and how do they differ from mine?
- Before finalizing a decision, have I considered its impact beyond my immediate team?
- What one conversation can I initiate to better understand how another function operates and connects with mine?

# Chapter 9

## Thinking in Terms of Trade-Offs

One of the most defining characteristics of strategic thinking is the recognition that choices involve trade-offs. In everyday work, it is tempting to believe that with enough effort, collaboration, or efficiency, every desirable outcome can be achieved simultaneously—high quality, low cost, rapid delivery, minimal risk, and maximum flexibility. In practice, however, resources are limited, time is finite, and priorities compete. The ability to think clearly about trade-offs distinguishes thoughtful decision-making from reactive action.

In task-oriented work, individuals often attempt to fulfill every request equally. When confronted with competing demands, they may try to accommodate all expectations without acknowledging the inherent tension between them. This approach can lead to overcommitment, diluted focus, and inconsistent results. Strategic thinking, by contrast, accepts that not all objectives can be maximized at the same time. It requires identifying what must take precedence and what may need to be adjusted or deferred.

Consider a project with an aggressive deadline and high quality expectations. Attempting to deliver both perfectly may strain capacity or introduce stress across the team. A trade-off perspective would involve asking: If time is constrained, should we reduce scope? If quality is non-negotiable, should we extend timelines or allocate additional resources? Recognizing these choices explicitly helps prevent unrealistic expectations and clarifies priorities for all stakeholders.

Trade-offs also appear in more subtle forms. For example, responding immediately to every stakeholder request may enhance short-term responsiveness but reduce time available for strategic planning or deep analysis. Investing heavily in innovation may accelerate future growth but temporarily increase costs or operational complexity. Prioritizing standardization may improve efficiency but reduce flexibility. Strategic thinking involves evaluating these tensions thoughtfully rather than defaulting to whichever pressure feels strongest in the moment.

A key step in developing trade-off awareness is making implicit choices explicit. Often, teams act as though all goals can be pursued simultaneously, only to experience conflict or disappointment when outcomes fall short. By articulating trade-offs openly—acknowledging what will be emphasized and what will be deprioritized—individuals and teams create clarity. This clarity reduces confusion and strengthens alignment because everyone understands the rationale behind decisions.

Another important dimension of trade-offs is time horizon. Some decisions prioritize short-term gains at the expense of long-term stability, while others invest in future benefits that may not yield immediate results. Strategic thinking requires balancing these horizons. It involves asking whether today's efficiency might create tomorrow's constraint, or whether short-term discomfort could lead to long-term resilience.

For example, investing time in documenting processes may feel burdensome when immediate deadlines loom. However, failing to document may result in repeated errors or onboarding challenges later. By evaluating the trade-off between short-term convenience and long-term sustainability, individuals can make more informed choices about where to allocate effort.

Trade-offs also shape collaboration across functions. One team's gain may require another team's adjustment. Recognizing this dynamic encourages empathy and negotiation rather than unilateral decision-making. When individuals understand that every choice influences multiple dimensions of performance, they become more deliberate in seeking input and building consensus around priorities.

Importantly, thinking in terms of trade-offs does not mean becoming indecisive. On the contrary, it strengthens decisiveness by grounding choices in clear reasoning. When trade-offs are acknowledged, decisions are less likely to be revisited repeatedly because their implications have been considered in advance. This builds confidence and credibility, particularly in environments where resources and expectations are constantly shifting.

Over time, individuals who consistently recognize and articulate trade-offs are seen as mature and balanced thinkers. They avoid overpromising, anticipate tensions, and help others understand the consequences of competing demands. Their decisions reflect awareness of complexity rather than an attempt to satisfy every expectation simultaneously.

Ultimately, thinking in terms of trade-offs is about accepting that strategy involves choice. It is about understanding that saying "yes" to one priority often requires saying "not now" to another. By developing comfort with these choices and communicating them transparently, individuals strengthen their ability to contribute thoughtfully to organizational direction and performance.

**Practice Prompts: Thinking Beyond the Task**

- What competing priorities are present in this situation?
- If I choose to emphasize one objective, what might need to be reduced or postponed?

- Am I trying to satisfy all demands without acknowledging inherent tensions?
- What are the short-term and long-term implications of this decision?
- How can I communicate trade-offs clearly so others understand the reasoning behind the choice?

# Chapter 10

## From Solving Today's Problem to Preventing Tomorrow's

In many organizations, the rhythm of work is shaped by problem-solving. Issues arise, teams respond, and operations continue. When problems are resolved quickly, it creates a sense of momentum and competence. However, when similar issues recur repeatedly, individuals may find themselves trapped in cycles of correction rather than progress. Strategic thinking begins to mature when the focus shifts from solving today's problem to preventing tomorrow's.

A task-oriented mindset approaches problems as isolated events. Once the immediate issue is addressed, attention moves to the next demand. While this approach maintains short-term continuity, it often leaves underlying patterns untouched. Over time, recurring disruptions consume increasing amounts of energy and attention, reducing the capacity to focus on growth, innovation, or long-term priorities.

Consider a team that frequently encounters errors in client documentation. Each time an error appears, it is corrected and resent. The immediate issue is resolved, and work proceeds. Yet if the same type of error surfaces repeatedly, it signals that the root cause has not been examined. Perhaps instructions are unclear, templates are inconsistent, or review processes are insufficient. Without investigating these possibilities, the team remains reactive.

Preventing tomorrow's problems requires stepping back from the urgency of correction and asking broader questions. Why does this issue keep emerging? What patterns can be observed across occurrences? Are there structural factors—such as unclear processes, misaligned incentives, or communication gaps—that contribute to recurrence? By exploring these dimensions, individuals shift from treating symptoms to addressing causes.

This shift does not always demand extensive analysis. Often, it begins with noticing patterns and initiating conversations. For example, after resolving a recurring operational issue, a team member might suggest a brief review to identify common triggers. Such reflection may reveal simple adjustments—clarifying roles, revising checklists, or improving handoffs—that significantly reduce future disruptions.

Another element of prevention involves anticipating risks before they materialize. Strategic thinkers develop sensitivity to early warning signs: small inconsistencies, repeated misunderstandings, or emerging constraints that could escalate if ignored. By addressing these signals early, they reduce the likelihood of larger problems later. This proactive orientation strengthens stability and builds confidence among colleagues and stakeholders.

Preventing tomorrow's problems also requires balancing immediate delivery pressures with time invested in improvement. In fast-paced environments, teams may feel they cannot afford to pause for reflection. Yet failing to allocate even small intervals for reviewing patterns can lead to greater inefficiency over time. Strategic thinking involves recognizing that prevention, though sometimes less visible than rapid correction, ultimately conserves resources and enhances performance.

Communication plays a vital role in this process. Sharing insights about recurring issues and proposing preventive measures transforms individual awareness into collective learning. Rather than simply reporting that a problem has been fixed, individuals can highlight trends and recommend adjustments. This shifts conversations from "How do we respond?" to "How do we improve?" Over time, such contributions strengthen a culture of continuous refinement rather than repeated firefighting.

Importantly, prevention is not about eliminating all uncertainty or risk. Complex environments will always produce unexpected challenges. The goal is not perfection but resilience—creating processes and habits that reduce avoidable disruptions and enable quicker recovery when unforeseen events occur. Strategic thinking supports this resilience by encouraging foresight and pattern recognition.

Individuals who consistently move from reactive correction to proactive improvement often gain increased trust and influence. They are seen as contributors who think about sustainability, not just immediate relief. Their work supports stability and long-term effectiveness, qualities that are essential for leadership readiness.

Ultimately, the transition from solving today's problem to preventing tomorrow's represents a deeper stage of strategic thinking. It reflects a commitment to understanding systems, recognizing patterns, and investing in improvements that extend beyond the present moment. By cultivating this habit, everyday work becomes less about managing recurring disruptions and more about shaping conditions for sustained success.

**Practice Prompts: Thinking Beyond the Task**

- Has this problem occurred before, and if so, what patterns can I identify?
- What underlying factors might be contributing to this recurring issue?
- What small preventive step could reduce the likelihood of this problem in the future?

- How can I document or share insights so others benefit from this learning?
- Am I spending more time correcting issues than improving the process that creates them?

# PART IV

## Becoming Known as a Strategic Thinker

Strategic thinking begins as an internal shift—how you interpret tasks, prioritize work, anticipate consequences, and understand interdependencies. Over time, however, it becomes visible to others through how you communicate, influence, and reflect on your contribution. This final stage of development is not about acquiring authority or title; it is about consistently demonstrating perspective in ways that shape how others experience your work.

Many professionals think strategically in private but do not make that thinking visible. They reflect deeply, connect ideas, and consider implications, yet their communication remains limited to updates and execution details. As a result, colleagues may continue to perceive them primarily as reliable performers rather than as contributors of insight. Becoming known as a strategic thinker requires translating internal perspective into external clarity.

This transition begins with communication. Strategic thinkers move beyond reporting what has been done and begin to articulate what it means. They connect actions to outcomes, highlight trade-offs, and frame decisions within broader goals. Instead of simply stating progress, they provide context. Instead of presenting data alone, they interpret it. These subtle shifts signal that their thinking extends beyond immediate deliverables.

Influence is another dimension of visibility. Strategic thinkers do not wait for formal authority to contribute perspective. They use thoughtful questions, clear reasoning, and collaborative framing to shape discussions and decisions. They are attentive to how their ideas are received and adjust their approach to align with different stakeholder concerns. This capacity to influence without relying on hierarchy strengthens their credibility and expands their impact.

Reflection also plays a central role. Strategic thinking develops through ongoing review of experiences—examining what worked, what did not, and what patterns are emerging. Individuals who regularly engage in such reflection refine their judgment and strengthen their ability to anticipate future implications. Over time, this reflective habit becomes a quiet but powerful engine of growth.

In this final part of the book, the focus shifts from perspective alone to presence—how strategic thinking is expressed in communication, influence, and daily habits. You will explore how to communicate insights rather than just updates, how to influence outcomes without formal authority, and how to cultivate a practice of reflection that sustains long-term development.

The aim is not to transform personality or adopt a new style. It is to make visible the perspective you are developing. When others consistently experience your contributions as thoughtful, context-aware, and forward-looking, they begin to associate you with strategic maturity. Opportunities for greater responsibility often follow not because you seek them directly, but because your way of engaging with work signals readiness.

Strategic thinking, ultimately, is not only about how you interpret work but also about how your interpretation shapes conversations, decisions, and relationships. By integrating perspective with communication and reflection, you move from thinking strategically in isolation to being recognized as someone who strengthens the strategic capacity of the teams around you.

# Chapter 11

## Communicating Insights, Not Just Updates

In many professional environments, communication is centered around updates. Reports describe what has been completed, meetings summarize progress, and emails confirm actions taken. This type of communication is essential for coordination and accountability. However, when communication remains limited to updates alone, opportunities to contribute strategic insight may be missed.

Being known as a strategic thinker requires more than performing well; it requires communicating in a way that reflects perspective. The distinction between updates and insights is subtle but powerful. An update answers the question, "What happened?" An insight answers the question, "What does it mean, and what should we consider next?"

Consider a project review meeting. A task-focused contribution might sound like: "The implementation phase is 80% complete, and testing will begin next week." This update provides useful information, but it does not shape the conversation. A more strategic contribution might be: "The implementation phase is 80% complete. Based on current progress, we may face capacity constraints during testing if additional support is not arranged. It would be helpful to confirm resource availability now to avoid delays."

The second statement does not merely report status; it interprets implications and anticipates future impact. It signals awareness of context and encourages proactive decision-making.

Communicating insights begins with asking yourself a simple question before sharing information: "What is the implication of this information?" Instead of transmitting data in isolation, you consider how it connects to priorities, risks, trade-offs, or long-term objectives. Even a brief reflection can transform routine updates into meaningful contributions.

Another important element is clarity of framing. Strategic communication often follows a simple structure: context, observation, implication, and recommendation. For example:

- Context: "Customer complaints have increased over the past two weeks."
- Observation: "Most complaints relate to delayed responses."
- Implication: "If this pattern continues, customer satisfaction scores may decline."
- Recommendation: "We may need to review response workflows or allocate temporary support."

This structure ensures that information is not only presented but also interpreted. It demonstrates that you are thinking beyond immediate facts and considering broader outcomes.

Tone also matters. Strategic communication is not about sounding authoritative or definitive. It is about presenting perspective thoughtfully and inviting dialogue. Phrases such as "It may be worth considering…" or "One potential implication is…" maintain openness while still contributing valuable insight. This approach reduces defensiveness and encourages collaborative refinement of ideas.

Communicating insights requires preparation. Before meetings or reports, take time to reflect on the broader context of your work. What are the key objectives currently guiding the team? What risks are emerging? Where might dependencies create friction? With this awareness, your contributions naturally extend beyond updates into analysis and foresight.

Over time, colleagues begin to notice patterns in how you communicate. If your updates consistently include thoughtful interpretation and forward-looking considerations, you become associated with strategic awareness. Managers may seek your input earlier in decision processes because they recognize your ability to connect details with broader implications.

Importantly, communicating insights does not mean offering commentary on every topic. Discernment is essential. Strategic thinkers choose moments where their perspective adds clarity or anticipates risk. This selectivity enhances credibility, as contributions are seen as purposeful rather than habitual.

The shift from updates to insights also changes how you experience your own work. Instead of viewing communication as a routine reporting requirement, you begin to see it as an opportunity to influence direction. Each interaction becomes a chance to connect tasks to outcomes and to elevate discussions beyond surface-level information.

Ultimately, strategic thinking becomes visible through communication that goes one step further—beyond what happened, toward what it means. By consistently sharing insights alongside updates, you demonstrate not only competence in execution but also maturity in interpretation. This visible integration of action and awareness is what gradually establishes you as someone who thinks beyond the task.

### Practice Prompts: Thinking Beyond the Task

- Before sharing an update, have I reflected on its broader implications?
- What might this information mean for upcoming decisions or priorities?

- Can I offer a concise recommendation or next step along with the update?
- Am I framing my communication in a way that connects details to larger goals?
- After meetings or reports, did my contributions help clarify direction or anticipate challenges?

# Chapter 12

## Influencing Without Formal Authority

In many organizations, influence is often associated with hierarchy. Titles, reporting lines, and decision rights determine who formally approves initiatives and sets direction. Yet strategic thinking is not limited to those with positional authority. In fact, one of the clearest signs of maturity in professional development is the ability to influence outcomes thoughtfully and constructively without relying on title or power.

Many employees hesitate to contribute beyond execution because they believe influence belongs to managers. They may think, "It's not my place to shape this decision," or "I don't have the authority to suggest changes." While respecting formal structures is important, strategic contribution does not require overriding authority. It requires framing ideas in ways that help others see implications, risks, and opportunities more clearly.

Influence without authority begins with credibility. When your work is reliable and your thinking demonstrates awareness of context, others are more receptive to your input. Execution builds trust; perspective deepens it. Over time, this combination allows you to contribute ideas that shape direction, even if final decisions rest elsewhere.

One of the most effective ways to influence is through framing. Instead of presenting an idea as a personal preference, align it with shared objectives. For example, rather than saying, "I think we should delay this launch," you might say, "Given our goal of maintaining quality standards, it may be helpful to review testing capacity before confirming the launch date." By connecting the suggestion to a widely accepted objective, you position the idea within the organization's priorities rather than as an individual opinion.

Questions are another powerful influence tool. As discussed earlier, thoughtful questions can elevate discussion without confrontation. Asking, "How might this affect our other ongoing commitments?" invites reflection without directly opposing a proposal. Such questions subtly shape thinking and often lead decision-makers to reconsider assumptions on their own.

Timing also plays a critical role. Influence is more effective when offered early in discussions rather than after decisions have been finalized. Preparing in advance, understanding agendas, and anticipating potential concerns allow you to contribute at moments when direction is still being shaped. Waiting until implementation is underway may reduce the opportunity for meaningful impact.

Another important aspect of influence is empathy. Understanding the pressures, constraints, and objectives faced by others increases the likelihood that your contributions will be received constructively. When you frame suggestions in ways that acknowledge these realities—rather than ignoring them—you demonstrate awareness of the broader system. This strengthens relationships and enhances the credibility of your perspective.

Influencing without authority also requires emotional composure. Not every suggestion will be accepted. Strategic thinkers recognize that influence is cumulative. Even when ideas are not adopted immediately, consistently offering thoughtful, well-framed insights builds a reputation for perspective and balance. Over time, this reputation often leads to greater inclusion in key conversations.

Importantly, influence is not about persuasion at any cost. It is about contributing to better decisions. When your intention is aligned with collective success rather than personal recognition, your communication naturally reflects collaboration rather than competition. This orientation fosters trust and makes influence more sustainable.

As individuals develop the ability to influence without formal authority, their professional identity begins to shift. They move from seeing themselves solely as implementers to viewing themselves as contributors to direction and outcomes. This shift does not require a change in title; it requires confidence in perspective and clarity in communication.

Ultimately, strategic thinking gains impact when it shapes collective action. By learning to influence thoughtfully—through framing, questioning, empathy, and timing—you extend the reach of your perspective beyond your immediate tasks. In doing so, you demonstrate that strategic contribution is not defined by hierarchy but by the quality of insight and the manner in which it is shared.

**Practice Prompts: Thinking Beyond the Task**

- How can I frame my suggestion in terms of shared goals rather than personal opinion?
- What questions could help others see broader implications without creating defensiveness?
- Am I offering input at a stage when decisions are still open to refinement?
- What pressures or constraints might the decision-maker be facing?
- Over time, how can I build credibility so that my perspective is sought more frequently?

# Chapter 13

## Developing a Habit of Strategic Reflection

Strategic thinking does not develop solely through exposure to complex situations. It strengthens through reflection—through the deliberate act of reviewing experiences, examining decisions, and identifying patterns. Without reflection, even meaningful insights may fade quickly, replaced by the urgency of the next task. With reflection, everyday experiences become learning opportunities that refine judgment and deepen perspective over time.

In fast-paced work environments, reflection is often overlooked. Days conclude with incomplete to-do lists, unanswered emails, and preparations for the following morning. Pausing to think about what was learned or how decisions influenced outcomes may feel secondary to immediate demands. Yet it is precisely this pause that converts experience into strategic growth.

Strategic reflection involves asking questions that extend beyond performance metrics. Instead of focusing only on whether tasks were completed, it explores how choices were made and what consequences followed. What assumptions guided a decision? Were trade-offs clearly recognized? Did communication highlight implications effectively? What patterns are emerging across similar situations? By engaging with such questions, individuals sharpen their awareness of how their thinking influences results.

Consider the end of a week filled with competing priorities. Rather than simply noting which deadlines were met, a strategic reflection might examine how priorities were determined. Were urgent demands allowed to overshadow important long-term work? Were certain trade-offs made repeatedly? Did any preventable problems recur? This analysis does not aim to assign blame but to identify patterns that can inform future choices.

Reflection also enhances anticipation. When individuals consistently review past decisions and outcomes, they develop a richer mental model of how events unfold within their organization. This model improves their ability to foresee consequences and recognize early warning signs in new situations. Over time, anticipation becomes more intuitive because it is grounded in accumulated insight.

Developing a habit of reflection does not require extensive journaling or long periods of analysis. Even brief, structured pauses can be effective. For example, at the end of a day or week, setting aside five to ten minutes to consider a few guiding questions can significantly strengthen awareness. The key is consistency. Regular reflection builds cumulative learning that occasional deep analysis cannot replace.

Another powerful approach is reflective dialogue. Discussing experiences with colleagues or mentors can reveal perspectives that might otherwise remain unnoticed. Such conversations encourage examination of assumptions and provide alternative interpretations of events. In this way, reflection becomes both an individual and collective practice, reinforcing strategic capacity across teams.

Importantly, strategic reflection includes acknowledging successes as well as challenges. When a decision leads to a positive outcome, exploring why it was effective helps reinforce good judgment. Identifying which factors contributed to success clarifies patterns worth repeating. This balanced approach prevents reflection from becoming overly critical and instead positions it as a tool for continuous improvement.

Over time, the habit of reflection transforms how individuals engage with work. They become less reactive and more deliberate, recognizing that each experience contributes to a larger learning trajectory. Mistakes are viewed as information rather than failure, and successes as insights rather than coincidence. This orientation fosters resilience and adaptability, qualities essential for navigating complex organizational environments.

As reflection deepens, strategic thinking becomes less effortful. Instead of consciously applying principles in every situation, individuals begin to respond with intuitive awareness shaped by accumulated experience. Decisions reflect pattern recognition, sensitivity to trade-offs, and anticipation of consequences. What once required deliberate analysis gradually becomes an integrated way of engaging with work.

Ultimately, developing a habit of strategic reflection completes the journey from task-focused execution to sustained strategic contribution. It ensures that everyday experiences continuously refine judgment and expand perspective. Through consistent reflection, you not only think beyond the task—you strengthen your capacity to do so with greater clarity and confidence over time.

**Practice Prompts: Thinking Beyond the Task**

- At the end of this week, what key decisions did I make, and what influenced them?
- Were there recurring patterns in the problems or priorities I faced?
- What trade-offs did I navigate, and how effectively were they communicated?
- What worked particularly well, and why?
- What one insight from this week can guide my approach next week?

# Beyond Work

## The Wider Reach of Strategic Thinking

This book has explored strategic thinking within the context of everyday work. Yet the habits it encourages are not confined to professional roles. They arise from a broader orientation toward life itself — an attentiveness to consequence, connection, and conscious choice.

Strategic thinking, at its essence, is not about position or power. It is about perspective.

When perspective deepens, its influence quietly extends beyond the workplace.

### Anticipating Consequence: Living With Foresight

In organizations, anticipating consequences prevents recurring disruption and improves decision quality. In life, it shapes direction.

Most meaningful outcomes are rarely the result of single dramatic decisions. They are the accumulation of small, repeated choices — what we prioritize, what we postpone, what we tolerate, what we invest in. Health, trust, financial stability, and personal growth evolve gradually, shaped by patterns that often go unnoticed in the moment.

To pause before acting and ask, *What might this lead to over time?* is a subtle but transformative discipline. It introduces intention into daily living. It invites us to see not only the immediate comfort of a choice, but its unfolding trajectory.

In this way, strategic thinking becomes a practice of foresight — not prediction, but awareness of direction.

**Recognizing Trade-Offs: Choosing With Clarity**

No organization can optimize every variable simultaneously. Neither can an individual. Time, attention, energy, and resources are finite.

Every "yes" quietly contains a "not now."
Every gain in one area may require restraint in another.

When trade-offs are ignored, life feels conflicted and reactive. When trade-offs are acknowledged, choices become deliberate. Clarity replaces internal tension. Instead of attempting to satisfy competing impulses at once, one begins to choose in alignment with long-term priorities and personal values.

This acceptance of limitation is not restrictive. It is liberating. It allows focus to replace fragmentation.

## Seeing Systems: Understanding Patterns

In earlier chapters, we explored how work functions as a system — interconnected, dynamic, and shaped by repeated behaviors. Life operates in much the same way.

Relationships are formed through patterns of communication.
Reputation grows through consistent behavior.
Confidence strengthens through accumulated effort.
Financial security develops through habits rather than isolated actions.

To see life systemically is to recognize that small, consistent behaviors carry more weight than occasional intensity. It shifts attention from isolated events to evolving patterns.

Strategic thinking, then, becomes an awareness of trajectory — noticing where habits are leading rather than focusing only on where we stand today.

## Reflection: Turning Experience Into Wisdom

Experience alone does not guarantee growth. Reflection does.

Without reflection, days pass quickly and lessons dissolve into routine. With reflection, experience is examined, patterns are identified, and judgment is refined. A brief moment of pause — at the end of a day, a week, or a season — can convert activity into insight.

What shaped my decisions?
What patterns are emerging?
Where am I drifting, and where am I moving deliberately?

Such questions cultivate inner clarity. Over time, this clarity strengthens not only professional competence but personal direction.

**Thinking Beyond the Immediate**

Strategic thinking is ultimately a discipline of seeing beyond the surface of the present moment. It asks not only, *What must be done now?* but also, *What is unfolding because of this?*

In work, this discipline elevates contribution.
In life, it deepens intentional living.

To think beyond the task is to think beyond immediacy — to recognize that actions accumulate, choices shape direction, and patterns determine outcomes.

When this awareness becomes habitual, both work and life are approached with greater steadiness. Decisions feel less reactive, more deliberate. Effort feels less scattered, more aligned.

And slowly, almost quietly, perspective becomes practice — not only in what you do, but in how you choose to live.

# Epilogue

## A Way of Seeing

Across these pages, strategic thinking has been described through tasks, meetings, priorities, trade-offs, systems, and reflection. Yet beneath these practical applications lies something simpler and more enduring.

Strategic thinking is a way of seeing.

It is the ability to look beyond the surface of activity and notice direction.
To move beyond urgency and recognize importance.
To see not only what is happening, but what is gradually taking shape.

In everyday work, this way of seeing transforms execution into contribution. A task becomes part of a larger objective. A decision becomes a shaping force. A conversation becomes an opportunity to influence clarity. Over time, small moments of awareness accumulate, and perspective deepens almost without notice.

But this evolution is not dramatic. It does not arrive with a title change or formal recognition. It develops quietly — through repeated pauses before action, thoughtful acknowledgment of trade-offs, curiosity about patterns, and consistent reflection on experience.

Strategic maturity is less about authority and more about orientation.

When orientation shifts, work begins to feel different. Instead of reacting to demands, you begin to interpret them. Instead of simply solving problems, you begin to anticipate them. Instead of completing tasks, you begin to shape outcomes.

And something subtle changes internally as well. Clarity replaces haste. Intention replaces impulse. Patterns become visible. Choices feel grounded rather than pressured.

The invitation of this book has never been to add another responsibility to your workload. It has been to change the lens through which you approach what is already before you.

Tomorrow, you will receive new tasks. You will attend meetings. You will face competing demands and imperfect information. None of that will change.

What can change is how you see.

Will you respond only to what is immediate, or will you consider what is emerging?
Will you focus only on completion, or on contribution?
Will you act only for the moment, or with awareness of trajectory?

Strategic thinking is not a destination. It is a practice — renewed daily, strengthened through reflection, and refined through experience.

In every assignment, every decision, every conversation, the opportunity remains the same:

Not merely to do the work,
but to see beyond it.

# Strategic Thinking

## 10 Reminders

Strategic thinking is not a title. It is a discipline practiced in everyday moments. The following reminders summarize the habits explored throughout this book.

### 1. Connect Tasks to Outcomes

Before beginning any assignment, ask: *What larger objective does this support?*
Execution gains meaning when aligned with purpose.

### 2. Prioritize by Impact, Not Noise

Urgency is visible. Importance is not always. Choose based on long-term contribution, not immediate pressure.

### 3. Acknowledge Trade-Offs

Every decision emphasizes something and reduces something else.
Clarity improves when trade-offs are made explicit.

### 4. Anticipate Consequences

Small actions create future patterns.
Pause to consider what today's decision may shape tomorrow.

### 5. See Interdependencies

Your work does not stand alone.
Understand how your outputs become inputs for others.

### 6. Solve Root Causes

Fixing symptoms restores flow.
Addressing causes builds stability.

### 7. Ask Questions That Elevate Discussion

Thoughtful questions reveal assumptions, risks, and connections.
Strategic influence often begins with inquiry.

### 8. Communicate Implications, Not Just Information

Move beyond updates.
Highlight what the information means and what it suggests next.

### 9. Influence Through Alignment

Frame ideas around shared objectives.
Strategic contribution does not require formal authority.

### 10. Reflect Consistently

Experience becomes insight through reflection.
Review patterns. Refine judgment. Strengthen foresight.

**A Final Perspective**

Strategic thinking is practiced not in rare moments of grand decision-making, but in daily choices—how tasks are interpreted, how priorities are set, how conversations are shaped, and how lessons are absorbed.

The opportunity remains constant:

Not merely to complete the work,
but to contribute with awareness of direction.